Do these activities to prepare your child to read this book.

Does It Fit?

Help your child read these words out loud.
Then say, *Some of these words have the same sound at the beginning. Cross out three words that have a different beginning sound.*

many	that	heaven
hairs	his	count

See It, Say It

Ask your child to color the star beside the word when he or she finds it in the book.
Make sure your child understands what each word means.

⭐ birthday   ⭐ again

⭐ born   ⭐ numbers

To, With, and By

To	Read four pages out loud *to* your child. Run your finger under the words as you say them at a normal speed. Make sure your child is looking at the words.
With	Read the same four pages out loud *with* your child. Run your finger under the words as you say them at a normal speed. Your child will probably say every other word correctly.
By	Run your finger under the words as your child says them *by* himself or herself. Help your child fix any mistakes.

Continue doing *To, With, and By* a few pages at a time for the rest of this book. Have your child reread this story for the next several days until it sounds great and is practically memorized.

 Go to www.RocketReaders.com for more reading tips.

Faith Kidz® is an imprint of Cook Communications Ministries
Colorado Springs, Colorado 80918
Cook Communications, Paris, Ontario
Kingsway Communications,
Eastbourne, England

WHY DID JESUS SAY THAT?
©2004 by Peggy Wilber

First printing, 2004
Printed in Korea
1 2 3 4 5 6 7 8 9 10 Printing/Year 08 07 06 05 04

Senior Editor: Heather Gemmen
Design Manager: Jeffrey P. Barnes
Designer: Kelly Robinson

Library of Congress Cataloging-in-Publication Data

Wilber, Peggy M.
  Why did Jesus say that? / written by Peggy Wiiber ; illustrated by
Terry Julien.
      p. cm. -- (Rocket readers. Level 4)
Summary: Easy-to-read format explores four metaphors that Jesus used to
teach lessons as described in the Bible's New Testament.
  ISBN 0-7814-3995-7 (pbk.)
  1. Jesus Christ--Words--Juvenile literature. 2. Jesus
Christ--Juvenile literature. [1. Jesus Christ--Parables. 2. Parables.]
I. Julien, Terry, ill. II. Title. III. Series.
  BT306.W54 2004
  232.9'54--dc22
                                        2003016478

Why Did Jesus Say That?

Rocket Readers Level 4

Written by

Peggy Wilber

Illustrated by

Terry Julien

Chapter 1

Mark 10:25

Jesus said,
"It is hard for a camel
to go through a needle.
It is harder for a rich man
to go to heaven."
Why did he say that?

Did Jesus like camels
more than people?

Or did a rich man like money
more than God?

Jesus told a rich man,
"Give your money away.
Then go with me."

The rich man liked his money.
He did not go with Jesus.

Chapter 2

John 10:14

Jesus said,
"I am the good shepherd."
Why did he say that?

Did he need a job?
Did he take care of sheep?

Did he need a sweater?
Or does he take care of us
like a shepherd takes care of sheep?

Jesus loves us
like a shepherd loves his sheep.

Jesus loves us.
He will always keep us safe.

Chapter 3

Luke 12:7

Jesus said,
"Your hairs are counted."
Why did he say that?

Did he like to count?

Did he love big numbers?

Did he like hair?

Or does he love us?

Jesus knows us.
He knows how many hairs we have.

Jesus loves you.
Jesus counts your hairs.
You can count on him.

Chapter 4

John 3:7

Jesus said,
"You must be born again."
Why did he say that?

Did Jesus like birthday cake?

Do people need two birthdays?

Did Jesus like presents?

Or do we need new life from him?

A man said to Jesus,
"I want to go to heaven."
Jesus said, "You must be born again."

When you trust in Jesus,
you get new life from him.
You will be born again.

Why Did Jesus Say That?

Life Issue: I want my child to know that God is faithful to us.

Spiritual Building Block: Faithfulness

Help your child learn about God's faithfulness in the following ways:

Sight: Have your child look at the picture on pages 6–7 for twenty seconds. Close the book and ask your child to list as many items as he or she can remember in the picture. Let your child look at the picture again to see what items were missed. Now look at a different picture and see how many items you can remember.

Sound: Say two words to describe God. For example: *God is kind and faithful.* Ask your child to repeat the sentence and add a word. *God is kind, faithful, and big!* Then you say the sentence and add another word. Do this until someone forgets a word or says them out of order. (Your child may have to play this game several times to build up to remembering seven words that describe God.)

Touch: Ask your child to write this Bible verse from John 10:14 on the lines below:

Jesus said, "I am the good shepherd."